KANT IN 90 MINUTES

D1102807

53321

In the same series by the same author:

Plato in 90 minutes
Aristotle in 90 minutes
Descartes in 90 minutes
Locke in 90 minutes
Hume in 90 minutes
Nietzsche in 90 minutes
Wittgenstein in 90 minutes

Paul Strathern

KANT
(1724–1804)
in 90 minutes

Constable · London

First published in Great Britain 1996
by Constable and Company Limited
3 The Lanchesters, 162 Fulham Palace Road
London W6 9ER
Copyright © Paul Strathern 1996
The right of Paul Strathern to be identified as author
of this work has been asserted by him
in accordance with the Copyright,
Designs and Patents Act 1988
ISBN 0 09 476210 4
Set in Linotype Sabon by
Rowland Phototypesetting Ltd,
Bury St Edmunds, Suffolk
Printed in Great Britain by
St Edmundsbury Press Ltd,
Bury St Edmunds, Suffolk

A CIP catalogue record of this book
is available from the British Library

All translations are by the author.

Contents

Introduction and background to his
philosophy   7

Life and work   9

Afterword   53

Key quotations   64

Chronology of significant
philosophical dates   76

Introduction

Just because a thing is impossible, this doesn't mean someone won't try to do it. Kant not only tried, but succeeded in achieving the impossible. After Hume had destroyed philosophy, and all possibility of constructing a metaphysical system, Kant created the greatest metaphysical system of them all. His motive was to refute Hume, but fortunately he had only read Hume's *Enquiry Concerning Human Understanding*, not the more penetrating scepticism of his earlier *Treatise of Human Nature*. Had Kant read this, he might have produced no system. This would have been a great pity, and would have left an entire generation of nineteenth-century German philosophy professors without a job.

Kant's system is like Newton's idea of gravity. It's not the final answer, but it's close to how we still see the world. You won't go far wrong if you look at the world Kant's way. Hume's philosophy is essentially simplistic: it reduces our philosophical condition to the barren rock of solipsism. Kant, building on the deceptive sands of error, created a wonderful sandcastle of such ingenuity and complexity that it can keep you happily absorbed with your bucket and spade for your entire holiday.

It's difficult to know what to say about Kant's life. He didn't really have one (outside his head). Nothing whatsoever of any real interest happened to him. However, the description of a life of utter tedium need not be boring in itself – as was demonstrated by his contemporary Casanova, and more recently by Hemingway.

Life and work

Immanuel Kant was born on 22 April 1724 in the Baltic city of Königsberg. This was then the capital of the isolated German province of East Prussia (now Kaliningrad in Russia). Kant's ancestors had emigrated from Scotland in the previous century, and may well have been related to Andrew Cant, the notorious seventeenth-century Scottish preacher. Cant is said to have been the origin of the verb 'to cant' with regard to the use of jargon – a family trait which was to reappear with a vengeance in the philosopher.

At the time of Kant's birth East Prussia was recovering from the devastation of war and plague, which had reduced the population by over half. Kant grew up in an atmosphere of pious poverty. He was the fourth child of the family – which eventually included five sisters and one further brother. Kant's Scottish father was a cutter of leather straps, who jocularly claimed that he 'could never make both ends meet', either at home or at work. Kant always remained respectful of his likeable but financially harassed father, and as a child is said to have enjoyed watching him deftly cutting up pieces of leather for harnesses. Yet according to the philosophical psychologist Ben-Ami Scharftstein, in the light of his father's dexterity 'Kant's great clumsiness with his hands is therefore noteworthy'.

Whether or not this is the case, and what precisely it might be noteworthy of, the main early influence in Kant's life was undoubtedly his mother. Frau Kant was a wholly uneducated German woman who is said to have possessed great 'natural intelligence'. It was this which particularly influenced her son Immanuel – or Manelchen as she called him ('Little Manny'). Kant's mother would take him for walks in the countryside and tell him the names of the plants and flowers. At night she would show him the stars, naming them and their constellations. She was a pious woman, and her loving but austere ways also played a formative role in the shaping of her son's moral character. This dual insistence on facts and moral obligation was to remain with

Kant throughout his life and played a leading role in his philosophy. Kant's most celebrated remark, made over fifty years later, harks directly back to these early days with his mother: 'The starry heavens above and the moral law within fill the mind with an ever new and increasing admiration and awe, the more often and the more steadily we reflect.'

Kant was brought up in a strict Pietist atmosphere, and from the age of eight to sixteen went to the local Pietist school. Here his exceptional intelligence and keen thirst for learning quickly became irked with the endless religious instruction. This dislike of formal religion was to remain with him for the rest of his days (in mature life he never attended church). Despite this, Kant retained much of the Pietist outlook, with its belief in a simple lifestyle and adherence to strict morality.

In 1737 Kant's mother died, and received a pauper's burial. Kant was fourteen at the time, and has indicated that he experienced his first sexual stirrings around this period. Psychologists have suggested that the loss of his beloved mother at this stage of puberty caused him to feel guilty and repress his sexual feelings. Either this, or they simply withered away. Whatever the cause: from now on Kant was to live a life of sexual repression which assumed heroic proportions.

At the age of eighteen Kant was admitted to the University of Königsberg as a theological student. Initially he was given financial assistance by the local Pietist church, but he also helped support himself by giving tuition to some of his more backward colleagues. He soon grew bored with theology and began showing a strong interest in mathematics and physics. He read Newton, who opened his eyes to the philosophic implications of the new discoveries in science and the great advances being made in all parts of this field, from astronomy to zoology. Science based on experiment could only be accommodated in an Empiricist philosophy, i.e., one which based our knowledge of the world on experience.

In 1746, when Kant was twenty-two, his father died. Kant, his brother and his five younger sisters were left penniless. The youngest sisters were taken in by a Pietist family, while the older ones went to work as chambermaids. Kant applied unsuccessfully for a job at a local school, and was forced to leave the university without taking a degree.

For the next nine years Kant supported himself as a tutor to rich families in the surrounding countryside. For a while he was employed by the Count and Countess Keyserling (the aristocratic family which was later to produce the pseudo-philosopher Hermann Keyserling, whose uplifting but bogus ideas were to prove such a comfort to disillusioned society matrons after the First World War). Whenever Kant had a little extra cash he would send some of it to his less fortunate sisters, a habit he continued throughout his life. But apart from these gifts he maintained no personal contact with his family. This was not because of any snobbishness on his behalf, but is claimed to have been due to the 'natural austerity and objectivity of his character' which was to become a feature of his later life. Kant's five sisters were to continue living in Königsberg (a city with just 50,000 inhabitants) throughout the whole of Kant's life. Yet he met none of them for over twenty-five years. When one of his sisters finally came to visit him he didn't even recognize her. After it was explained to him who she was, he apologized to the rest of the company for her lack of culture. Kant may not have been a social snob, but he was renowned for his inability to tolerate fools. Even in his own family, it would seem.

Yet this incident raises a curious point. Kant's sister must surely have borne more than a passing resemblance to his mother: both intellectually and physically. She would even have been around the same age as Kant's mother when she brought him up. Does this mean that Kant's celebrated love for his mother had become so deep that he no longer recognized it? Suggestion has been made that Kant unconsciously resented the repressive nexus – facts, morality, sexual extinction – imposed on him by his mother. His inability to recognize his sister (or indeed have anything to do with her) may well have had something to do with this. But we have no way of knowing. (Kant's sheer lack of life has perversely attracted far more attention from psychologists than the *comparatively* normal life lived by other philosophers. Though in my view the entire notion of normality in this field is a moot point.)

Kant may have been indifferent towards his own family, but he appears to have enjoyed life amongst the rich families where he was employed as a tutor. His appearance was as much an oddity as his character. He was less than five foot tall, and his head was disproportionately large compared to his body. His frame suffered from a slight corkscrew twist, which made his left shoulder droop, his right shoulder curve back, and his head tend to lean to one side. Dressed in threadbare clothes and with hardly a pfennig to his name, he'd not exactly been the hit of the campus at the University of Königsberg (which was itself hardly a centre of cosmopolitan society). But now, kitted out by his employers in his elegant tutor's outfit, and encouraged to mingle with the family guests, Kant positively blossomed.

He soon developed a ready wit, acquired a veneer of sophisticated assurance, and became a mean hand at the card and billiard tables. When the family departed for their summer holidays in the country, Kant accompanied them, journeying almost fifty miles from Königsberg. (This was the furthest he was ever to travel from his provincial home city throughout his life.) But this period of *relative* elegance was only a phase.

In 1755, at the age of thirty-one, Kant was at last able to take his degree at the University of Königsberg, partly owing to the charity of a Pietist benefactor. This was late to be finishing a degree; and as we shall see, Kant was an unusually late developer. By this age almost all the other major philosophers had already begun formulating the ideas for which they would be remembered. Not until two decades later did Kant really start to produce original philosophy.

Kant was now able to take up a post at the university as a *privatdozent* (junior lecturer). This post he held for the next fifteen years, living a bachelor academic existence of unremitting industry. During this period Kant lectured mainly on mathematics and physics, and published treatises on a large range of scientific subjects. These included volcanoes, the nature of winds, anthropology, the causes of earthquakes, fire, the ageing of the earth, even the planets (which he predicted would all one day be inhabited, those furthest from the sun developing the species with the highest intelligence).

Yet Kant's natural bent was towards speculation. He continued to read widely in philosophy. In rationalistic philosophy his ideas were most influenced by Newton and Leibnitz. Newton's greatest achievements may have been in physics and mathematics, but in those days these subjects were still considered part of philosophy: as 'natural philosophy'. The full title of Newton's greatest work is *Philosophiae Naturalis Principia Mathematica* (The Mathematical Principles of Natural Philosophy). Kant studied Newton with sufficient thoroughness to propose a 'New Theory of Motion and Rest' which opposed Newton's view. The fact that he had misunderstood Newton is not the point. He was being led to speculate on systems which encompassed the universe, and was willing to question the greatest intellect of the era on his own ground.

According to Leibnitz the physical world of cause and effect proved the inner harmony of the world's moral purpose. Reading Leibnitz led Kant to see humanity as not only participating in nature, but over and above this participating in the ultimate purpose of the universe.

At the same time Kant's interest in the philosophy of science led him to read the Scottish philosopher Hume. Kant was impressed by Hume's insistence on experience as the basis of all knowledge. This squared with the scientific approach. However, Kant found himself troubled by the sceptical conclusions which Hume drew from his rigid Empiricism. According to Hume, all we experience is a sequence of perceptions – and this means that such notions as cause and effect, bodies and things, even the controlling hand of God the creator, are all mere suppositions or beliefs.

None of them is ever actually experienced.

Surprisingly, Kant was also struck by the emotional appeal of Rousseau. The first of the Romantics, Rousseau was the most unacademic of all philosophers, believing in personal expression through emotion more than rational thought. His advocacy of liberty was to prove a heady inspiration for the French Revolution. Kant may have been an essentially dry character, but there was something in Rousseau that touched a chord in his deeply suppressed emotions. Beneath the façade of the prim academic beat the heart of a closet Romantic – and this was later to become apparent in his philosophy. But for the time being all these disparate elements – Newton, Leibnitz, Hume, Rousseau – remained just that. Not until Kant found a way of reconciling and absorbing these influences would he be able to start producing original philosophy. And the enormity of such a task would take a long time.

Perhaps Kant became impatient – for there now occurs an odd episode. Instead of publishing another serious academic work, Kant wrote a curious satirical book called *Dreams of a Ghost-Seer elucidated by means of Metaphysical Dreams*. The 'ghost-seer' of the title is the Swedish visionary and mystic Swedenborg, famous for his descriptions of his lengthy travels through heaven and hell. In 1756 Swedenborg had published his eight-volume masterwork *Arcana coelestia* (The Secrets of Heaven). Unfortunately sales did not go well, and after ten years only four copies had been sold. One of these is now known to have been bought by Kant. These volumes of metaphysical mumbo-jumbo had a profound effect on Kant – enough to inspire him to write an entire book satirizing them. As Kant whimsically declares in his introduction: 'The author confesses with a certain humility that he was so simple-minded as to track down the truth of some tales of the sort mentioned. He found – as usual, where one has nothing to look for – he found nothing.' Yet it soon becomes evident that Kant's mockery of 'the worst visionary of them all' and 'sundry airy thought-worlds . . . hewn . . . out of fraudulent concepts' is not quite what it seems. Beneath his consistent raillery and expressions of intellectual contempt, there is an unmistakable element of profound seriousness in Kant's interest in Swedenborg. He longed to believe in metaphysics (even if not in quite such an extreme form), but his formidable intellectual development was beginning to close down this avenue.

Kant's writing style is notoriously prolix and difficult, but by all accounts his lectures were quite the opposite. His body was so short and twisted that only his bewigged head, with its prim precise features, was visible above the lectern. But this talking head was a font of wit, fascinating erudition and ideas. Kant's lectures were a great hit, and his fame soon spread, encouraged by his stream of treatises on scientific subjects. His celebrated summer lectures on geography always attracted crowds from outside the university. These continued for over thirty years, and established Kant as the first academic teacher of physical geography, despite the fact that throughout his life he never set eyes on a mountain, and may never even have seen the open sea (which was all of twenty miles away). Kant's vivid perceptive descriptions brought to life the wonders of the distant lands which he read about with such enthusiasm during the long winter evenings, when the freezing Baltic fog drifted in through the streets of remote provincial Königsberg.

Kant now also began delivering lectures on philosophy, and here it soon became apparent that he had journeyed far and wide through the hostile territories of ethics and epistemology, beyond the Ultima Thule of logic, and even into regions so remote from civilization as metaphysics (and had lived to tell the tale). Meanwhile the treatises on more amenable subjects, such as fireworks, military defence and the theory of the heavens, continued to pour from his pen. Yet despite this, Kant was twice refused a professorship at the University of Königsberg. The reasons for this are unclear, but one suspects an element of provincial snobbery. Or perhaps they just didn't like him. Either way, Kant certainly liked Königsberg. When he was offered the prestigious post of Professor of Poetry at the University of Berlin, he turned it down. (This has deprived us of the joy of reading Kant's criticism of the poets in a style of such ponderous complexity that it would surely have become essential Dadaist reading.)

Fortunately in 1770 the Königsberg university authorities relented, and Kant was appointed Professor of Logic and Metaphysics. Now, by the age of forty-six, he had grown increasingly critical of Leibnitz and his rationalistic disciples, who had become the dominant force in German philosophy.

Hume's Empiricism seemed undeniable, and reluctantly he even became convinced by Hume's scepticism. Objects, cause and effect, continuity, even the self, all these appeared to be fallacious notions. They remained beyond the reach of our experience, which was the only certain source of our knowledge. Kant accepted this, because it seemed to him intellectually irrefutable. But he was not happy with this barren state of affairs. There appeared to be no further room for philosophy to continue. Was this really the end?

Then one day, whilst he was studying

Hume's *Enquiry Concerning Human Understanding*, Kant 'awoke from his dogmatic slumbers'. In a flash of inspiration he saw how he could construct a system, and answer the destructive scepticism of Hume which had threatened to destroy metaphysics for ever.

For eleven years Kant published nothing, but continued working out his philosophy. Already he had begun living a life of extreme regularity, and during this period his regularity of habit began to achieve legendary status. In the words of Heine: 'Rising, coffee drinking, writing, lecturing, dining, walking, each had its set time. And when Immanuel Kant, in his grey coat, cane in hand, appeared at the door of his house, and strolled towards the small avenue of linden trees which is still called "The Philosopher's Walk", the neighbours knew that it was exactly half past three by the clock. So he promenaded up and down, during all seasons; and when the weather was gloomy, or the grey clouds threatened rain, his old servant Lampe was to be seen plodding anxiously after, with a large umbrella under his arm, like a symbol of Prudence.' Only on one famous occasion is Kant said to have broken this routine – on the day he started reading Rousseau's *Émile*, when he became so absorbed that he missed his walk in order to finish it. Only Rousseau's avowal of Romantic emotion could make him forget his routine. But such feelings were not enough to cause any serious break with the habits of a lifetime. Although Kant twice considered marriage during these years, on both occasions he took so long making up his mind that by the time he'd decided (in favour, on both occasions) one of the ladies had become married to someone else, and the other had moved to another city. Kant was not a man to be rushed into any rash decisions. Yet his admiration for Rousseau's Romantic ideas was not confined to theory. Years later, when many of Rousseau's ideas came to fruition with the outbreak of the French Revolution, Kant wept with joy – a rare sentiment in the fiercely conservative provincial Prussian city of Königsberg, and probably unique amongst its crusty university establishment.

In 1781 Kant finally published his *Critique*

of Pure Reason, which is generally regarded as his masterpiece. Yet not all were so enthusiastic. When Kant sent a copy of the manuscript to his friend Herz, it was eventually returned only half read. Herz claimed that to continue reading Kant's work any further would have been to court insanity. And you may well feel the same. In his *Critique of Pure Reason* Kant decided to dispense with many interesting arguments and concrete examples, for fear of making his work too long. Even so, in the translated version it runs to over 800 pages. And most of it is like this: 'The apodeictical proposition cogitates the assertorical as determined by these very laws of the understanding, consequently affirming as *a priori*, and in this manner it expresses . . .'

Even in the finest translation it only *sounds* better: '*La proposizione apodittica concepisce il guidizio assertorio determinato secondo queste legge dell'intelletto stresso e, per consequenza, come affirmativo a priori; ed esprime cosi* . . .' You just don't want to know what it's like in German (the miracle is that Herz managed to get as far as halfway before fearing for his sanity).

But don't let this distract you from the magnificence of Kant's actual system. His aim was to restore metaphysics. He agreed with Hume and the Empiricists that there are no such things as innate ideas; but he denied that all knowledge was derived from experience. The Empiricists stated that all knowledge must conform to experience; Kant brilliantly reversed this by saying that all experience must conform to knowledge. According to Kant space and time are subjective. They are our method of perceiving the world. In a way they are like irremovable spectacles, without which we are incapable of making sense of our experience. But these are not the only subjective elements which help us understand our experience. Kant explained that there are twelve 'categories' (as he called them) which we conceive of by means of our understanding working independently of experience. These categories include such things as quality, quantity and relation. These too are like irremovable spectacles. We cannot see the world in any other way than in terms of quality, quantity and so forth. But through these irremovable spectacles we can only see the phenomena of the world – we can never perceive the actual nuomena, the true reality which supports or gives rise to these phenomena.

It has been said that only a man who has never seen a mountain could possibly believe that space is not there outside us, but merely part of our perceptual apparatus. And common sense would seem to agree with this. But such gauche *ad hominem* objections are nothing to do with philosophy, so I have been told.

Space and time, and the categories (which include such notions as plurality, causality and existence) can only be applied to the phenomena of our experience. If we apply them to things which are not experienced, we end up with 'antinomies' – i.e., contrasting statements which can both apparently be proved by purely intellectual argument. In this way Kant demolishes all purely intellectual arguments for the existence (or non-

other him. He was fond of
e's remark: 'My friends, I
Indeed, he positively recom-
e. 'Friendship is a restriction
ntiments to a single subject,
sant to whomsoever they are
so a proof that generality and
cking.'

have claimed that Kant's
unwillingness) to form close
was indicative of a profound
ut Kant doesn't appear to have
Quite the opposite. Those who
ked on his cheerfulness. 'Kant's
as by nature meant for cheerful-
the world with a glad look ...
ed his cheerfulness to external
fore he was usually disposed to
as a typical observation by one
gues.

after the publication of his Cri-
Reason, Kant published his Cri-
Practical Reason. In this he
God, who was no longer deemed
e (because he didn't fit into the

existence) of God. We simply cannot apply such a category as existence to such a non-empirical entity.

As we can see, Kant was not in favour of a wholesale return to metaphysics in his *Critique of Pure Reason*. By 'pure reason' Kant here means *a priori* reason, i.e., something that can be known *prior* to experience. Hume had denied such transcendental entities (i.e., ones that 'transcend' experience). But Kant was convinced that he had restored this transcendental/metaphysical element to philosophy in the form of his 'categories of pure reason'. Hume's sceptical view may seem simplistic, and is certainly unworkable if we wish to live in the real world. (His denial of causality effectively reduces the whole of science to the status of metaphysics.) Kant's view, on the other hand, is immensely subtle and sophisticated – but it hardly overcomes Hume's point from a *philosophical* point of view. We may not be able to experience the world without conceiving of space, quantity and so forth. But it is difficult to argue that these are not an integral *part* of that experience, or to see how they could exist without it (i.e., prior to it).

On the other hand Kant's argument that we can never know the real world carries considerable weight. All the things we perceive are only phenomena. The thing-in-itself (the nuomena) which supports or gives rise to these phenomena remains for ever unknowable. And there is no reason why it should resemble *in any way* our perceptions. The phenomena are perceived by way of *our* categories, which have nothing whatsoever to do with the thing-in-itself. This remains beyond quality, quantity, relation and the like.

Meanwhile Kant continued to live his life of rigid routine. This did not preclude an element of socializing, though such activity was always very much a minor element in Kant's life. He maintained relations with a number of his brighter students, as well as a few members of the faculty. Yet he was never close with any of them. (No one was addressed with the informal '*du*', even after decades of social contact.) Thought was his life. 'For a scholar, thinking is a means of categories). The *Critique of Practical Reason* is devoted to the ethical part of Kant's system. Here, instead of seeking metaphysical grounds for our perception, he seeks them for our morality. Kant was searching for nothing less than the fundamental moral law. But surely it was impossible to discover such a law that would please everyone? From Christians to Buddhists, from liberals to Prussians – all believing in the same fundamental good? Kant believed it was possible to discover a basic law; but he did so by side-stepping what most would consider to be the main question. Good and evil were not his concern here. He wasn't seeking to discover some essence of all the different interpretations of these basic moral concepts. Kant stressed that he was seeking the *grounds* of morality, rather than its content. As with pure reason, so with practical reason: what was needed was a set of *a priori* principles like the categories.

In fact, Kant eventually came up with only one principle: his 'categorical imperative'. This was the *a priori* ground for all moral action: its metaphysical premiss. In an analogous way to the categories of pure reason, this gives a framework to our ethical thinking (practical reason), though without giving it any specific moral content. Kant's categorical imperative states: 'Act only in accord with a principle which you would at the same time will to be a universal law.'

This principle led Kant to believe that we should act in accordance with our duty, not according to our feelings. This resulted in some odd conclusions. For instance, Kant stated that the moral worth of an action should not be judged according to its consequences, but only insofar as it was done for the sake of duty. This is plainly daft – if morality is to do with society, rather than just individual self-righteousness.

Kant intended his categorical imperative as a mere framework, empty of moral content. But it isn't quite. It still contains traces of moral content. The morality of conformity, for a start. Kant's categorical imperative implies that everyone should act in precisely the same way, regardless of temperament or task. Should the head of a government act with the same moral scruples as the head of a monastery? Should he even try? Should Churchill have tried to behave like Gandhi? Or vice versa? Perhaps all systems are bound to lead to such rigidities. (But without any ethical system we'd be completely lost – unable to make any value judgements whatsoever.)

Kant's ethical system also led him to believe that we should never tell a lie, regardless of what consequences this might involve. He was well aware of the implications of this, but he stuck to it nonetheless. 'To tell a falsehood to a murderer, who is in pursuit of a friend of yours who has taken refuge in your house, would be a crime.'

Are we to believe that Kant would have delivered a Jewish friend to Nazis? No: everything we know about him convinces me that he would have followed the dictates of duty here. His highly active mind would quickly have discovered a duty which forbade him to hand over his friend.

Yet this question of never telling a lie exposes a distinct flaw in Kant's system. For make no mistake about it, Kant took this business about lies *extremely* seriously. He even spent time agonizing over the question of whether it was permissible to end a letter with the customary greeting of the period 'Your obedient servant'. Was this a lie? Kant insisted that he was no man's servant, and that he had no intention whatsoever of obeying his correspondents. But eventually he seems to have relented on this matter.

Yet on some more serious literary matters he remained unbending. Kant was against the reading of novels. They caused our thought to become 'fragmentary' and weakened our memory. 'For it would be ridiculous to memorize novels in order to relate them to others.' (The implication that Kant memorized all other books he read is not to be lightly dismissed.) Here Kant overlooks the fact that reading Rousseau's novel *Heloïse* was a formative experience, which he seems to have accomplished without exploding his thought into fragments or softening his memory.

Kant enjoyed reading poetry, but only if it was an intellectual harmonization of virtue and sentiment. Unrhymed poetry was simply prose gone mad. Music was a different, and altogether more difficult matter. This alone could penetrate the carapace of repression which protected his unexpressed emotions. And in consequence he was particularly harsh on it. Musicians were characterless because what they played reduced everything to feeling. He recommended his students to avoid listening to music because it would make them effeminate. Yet he couldn't stop attending concerts himself – until the day he attended one in memory of the philosopher Moses Mendelssohn. This struck him as nothing less than endless moaning, and he never attended a concert again. He detested folk music (such as his mother had often sung to him).

In 1790, at the age of fifty-eight, Kant published the third and final part of his monsterpiece, his *Critique of Judgement*. This is ostensibly concerned with aesthetic judgements, but also deals with theology (and much, much more). Kant argues that the existence of art presupposes the artist, and that it is through the beauty of the world that we recognize a benign creator. As he had previously implied, we recognize God's work in the stars of the heavens, as well as in our inner inclination to do good.

As with his theory of perception, and his ethical theory, Kant sought to establish a metaphysical basis to his theory of aesthetic judgement. He wished to establish an *a priori* principle which made our apprehension of beauty possible. Here Kant was on rather shakier ground. It's always difficult to get a consensus on beauty. Some consider the Swiss Alps pure chocolate-box, finding spiritual sustenance in Expressionism. Others do not. Such views are seemingly irreconcilable. But Kant was determined to bring *everything* within the bounds of his system.

Kant argues: 'A person who describes something as beautiful insists that everyone *ought* to give the object in question his approval.' The similarity to the categorical imperative is evident, but here it simply doesn't work – except in the personal pejorative sense. Once again we're faced with the conformity syndrome. Just because I find Francis Bacon's picture of a screaming pope beautiful, doesn't mean I expect everyone else to do so.

Kant goes on to argue that it is only through the unity and consistency of nature that science is possible. This unity cannot be proved, but must be assumed. Related to this idea is the notion that nature is purposive. Kant claims the purposiveness of nature is 'a special *a priori* concept'. As we now know, this concept is not necessary to an assumption of the unity and consistency of nature. And even the latter are now under question with Quantum Theory.

Kant insisted that although we can't prove the world has a purpose, we must look upon it 'as if' it has one. Kant didn't deny the evil, ugly and apparently purposeless aspects of the world, but he thought they counted for a lot less than their more uplifting opposites. In the next century, Schopenhauer was to take precisely the opposite point of view – with perhaps more justification. Though in the end neither the optimistic nor the pessimistic point of view can in any way be endorsed by proof, and remain ultimately a matter of temperament.

Meanwhile Kant continued with his indefatigable routine (which he pursued with a similar dedication to Casanova's endless womanizing and Hemingway's endless boozy big-game hunting, though scattering a lot less feathers in the process). And the citizens of Königsberg continued to set their watches according to when Kant started his afternoon walk: three-thirty p.m. *precisely.*

Kant's view that time is all in the mind, and has nothing to do with reality, may have had something to do with him living in East Prussia. This territory was surrounded to the south and the west by Poland, which lived one hour ahead of East Prussia. And over the eastern border was Russia, which was more than a week behind the rest of Europe. The nearest people who kept the same time as East Prussia were two borders away, across Poland to the west, in Germany.

Kant lived on Prinzessinnenstrasse, in a house which was demolished in 1893. Here he was looked after by his grumpy old servant Lampe, with whom he was capable of being equally grumpy. Everything had to be done exactly right (just like Casanova and Hemingway). Lampe even had to help his master out of his clothes each night in the correct order. And when Kant went to bed he invariably wore one night-cap in summer, and two in winter – which could be very cold indeed in Königsberg, when the nearby Baltic froze over.

In the manner of all pernickety domestic tyrants, Kant was always very concerned about Lampe's spiritual welfare. Indeed, Kant declared that he had reinstated God in his *Critique of Practical Reason* expressly in order to give Lampe something to believe in. Lampe may not have fully appreciated this: we have no evidence of his gratitude. Though it's a little easier to guess Lampe's attitude towards his master's unique philosophical method of holding up his stockings – by means of pieces of string which ran up through his trouser pockets and were attached to springs contained in two small boxes. (This last piece of information sounds utterly preposterous, but is confirmed by a number of independent sources, one of whom suggested that Kant's father being in the strap-making business had something to do with it. Whether or not this is significant continues to exercise the psychologists.)

Like many possessed of an independent and imaginative mind, Kant was a practising hypochondriac. Indeed, he was so good at it that he was the only person who ever noticed anything wrong with him. Throughout his long life this frail little man with the twisted frame was never known to be ill. His hypochondria involved him in a tireless and systematic regime: a critique of pure and practical physique. One of his habits was to breathe only through his nose, especially when he went on his walk in cold weather. This meant that during autumn, winter and spring he was incapable of replying to anyone who addressed him on the street, because he refused to open his mouth in case he caught a cold.

Kant was fortunate whilst publishing his three great *Critiques*. During this period the political situation in Prussia was unusually tolerant, not a quality often associated with that country. It is doubtful if Kant would have been able to publish such works in most other European countries. Kant appreciated this, and dedicated the *Critique of Pure Reason* to Zedlitz, Frederick the Great's minister of education. As befits a dry-as-dust provincial professor, Kant was outwardly respectful towards the king. But at heart he was surprisingly revolutionary. And he had nothing but contempt for the French philosophers who hung around Frederick's court. His particular *bête noire* was De la Mettrie, the charming author of such timeless philosophic classics as *Traité de l'Asthme et de la Dysenterie* and *Reflexions Philosophiques sur l'Origine des Animaux*, who sometimes wrote under the 'Chinese' pseudonym of Docteur Fum-Ho-Ham, and is said to have died '*pour une plaisanterie*' after eating an entire pheasant pâté in order to prove a point about indigestion to the German court doctors. Not exactly Kant's type.

But when Frederick the Great died in 1796

and Frederick William II ascended to the throne, Kant found himself in hot water. Wöllner, an ardent Pietist, took over at the Ministry of Education, and Kant was charged with misusing his philosophy to distort the Bible. Someone at the Ministry of Education had evidently managed to struggle through the 800 pages of the *Critique of Pure Reason*, and had discovered that it denied all proofs of the existence of God. Kant was required to give an undertaking that he would not deliver any lectures or write any further books on a religious subject. Kant wrote a letter to the king, giving his word that he would obey this order. But when the king died in 1797 Kant considered that he was released from his promise, and returned to the subject with renewed vigour. (As we see here, Kant's views on fibbing were indeed susceptible to adaptation, when the occasion arose.)

By now Kant was approaching seventy, and years of practice had perfected his hypochondria to the point where he was a master of this art. Each month he would send to the Königsberg chief of police for the latest mortality statistics, and from these he would calculate his own life expectancy. He became convinced that constipation clouded his brain, and added an impressive array of laxatives to his laboratory-sized medicine chest. Avidly he would read through the journals describing the latest medical discoveries, to determine whether he had any new diseases. Kant was undeniably a rarity. It is not often that man exhibits genius in both his life's work *and* his hobby. Alarmed faculty colleagues who attempted to dissuade him from his hobby were quickly put in their place. Kant knew far more about illness than any mere professor of medicine at the University of Königsberg. On this topic, as on all others, Kant could not tolerate contradiction. (Unlike other similarly afflicted egoists, he was invariably right, and he knew it.) As even an admirer was forced to concede: 'He cannot bear to hear others talk much, becomes impatient ... if anyone professes to know anything better than he does ... Direct contradiction insulted and – when it was persisted in – embittered him.' This was not entirely megalomania. Kant merely regarded the truth as sacrosanct. It wasn't his fault that he always knew what he was talking about, and others were often mistaken. 'He did not force his opinion on anyone, but reciprocal obstinacy caused him real grief.'

University professors may have been able to tolerate such treatment, but it proved too much for his servant Lampe, who had to put up with it *all the time*. After decades of faithful service Lampe eventually took to the bottle, and had to be dismissed.

Meanwhile Kant continued stoically resisting the attentions of his family. He continued to justify his lack of contact with his sisters by explaining that they weren't up to his intellectual level. (Since the death of Newton, it's probable that no one in Europe fulfilled this criterion.) When pressed further he said that they were pleasant enough, but he had nothing in common with them because they lacked culture. However, this excuse was certainly invalid with regard to his brother – who had grown to be a cultured professional man, but was equally ignored by Kant. This brother dearly longed for social contact with his famous philosophical sibling, and regularly wrote letters to him suggesting that they meet. But all to no avail. At one stage he pleaded to Kant: 'I can no longer bear that such separation should continue, we are brothers.' Kant often took as long as two years to reply to these letters, claiming that he had been too busy to write earlier. (Though he had of course managed to find time to write several hundred pages of mind-boggling philosophy.) At the age of sixty-eight, after a delay of two and a half years in replying to his brother's latest letter begging for a meeting, Kant wrote assuring him that he would bear his brother in his thoughts during the short period of life remaining to him, but carefully refrained from mentioning any meeting.

As he grew older Kant became increasingly solitary and misanthropic. 'Life is a burden to me,' he confessed at last, 'I am tired of bearing it. And if the angel of death were to come this night and call me from here, I would raise my hand and say, "God be praised!"' But he still continued avidly with his hobby, which was presumably intended to prolong his life. Any thought of putting an end to it all was dismissed. He was not afraid to commit suicide, but it was morally wrong. Increasingly he began suffering from nightmares. Each night in his sleep he would find himself surrounded by footpads, stalked by murderers. The paranoid symptoms are unmistakable. He declared: 'Everyone almost hates the other, tries to raise himself above his fellow men, is full of envy, jealousy, and other fiendish vices. Man is not a god, he is a devil.' He came to the conclusion that 'if a man were to say and write all he thinks, there would be nothing more horrible on God's earth than man'. These last two quotes are curiously revealing of how he must have viewed himself – at the end of a crotchety, but largely blameless life. (It wasn't his fault about Lampe, who could always have sought employment elsewhere. And he may not have seen his sisters, but he regularly sent them money.)

Kant's natural cheerfulness was now being

swamped by the rising tide of his suppressed emotional life. He was certainly unhappy, but he was determined to remain true to himself to the end. He insisted that he didn't mind being unhappy. This attitude is quite consistent with his philosophy. In the *Critique of Practical Reason* he had declared that he found it 'astonishing how intelligent men have thought of declaring happiness as a universal practical law'. In his view, happiness and morality had nothing essential to do with one another. We may be gratified when we perform an act of virtue, but he was unable to comprehend 'how a mere thought containing nothing sensuous can produce a sensation of pleasure or displeasure'. Such could only have been the expression of a mind utterly withdrawn from the emotions. (Even the driest of mathematicians admit their pleasure on arriving at a difficult solution.)

Yet Kant did admit to one experience which regularly gave him pleasure. His secret vice was characteristically solitary. He enjoyed watching the birds, and would wait impatiently for their return each spring.

According to a colleague: 'the one joy that nature still allowed him . . . was the return of a warbler that sang outside the window in his garden. Even in his joyless old age, this one joy remained to him. If his friend remained away too long, he said, "It must still be very cold on the Apennines."' Scharftstein, upon whose brilliantly perceptive sketch of Kant's life I have drawn heavily, suggests that the birds represented freedom for Kant. Yet freedom from what? The tyranny of his own nature, certainly. But also perhaps freedom from thought – that very element which he had allowed to enslave his life, the element with which he sought to imprison the entire world within his system.

For the last decade of his life Kant devoted himself to a mammoth philosophical work which he was never to finish. Kant intended to give this work the catchy title *Übergang von den metaphysische Anfangsgründe der Naturwissenschaft zur Physik* (Transition from the Metaphysical Foundations of Natural Science to Physics). Unlike Kant's earlier works, this is definitely unreadable. Bravely risking insanity, several experts have tried to scale this Everest of the German Metaphysical Himalayas, but have returned gasping for air and incapable of coherent communication. As far as we can gather from the survivors of this work, in it Kant advances his general *a priori* structure for a science of nature, showing in exhaustive detail how this can be extended to apply to particular sciences. The emphasis here is on the 'exhaustive detail'.

Kant now became a sad figure, his great faculties gradually failing. It is said that hypochondria is often a defence mechanism against paranoia. Yet despite diligent and exhaustive practice at his hobby, Kant's paranoia gradually began to get the upper hand. He started to experience pressure on his brain, which he decided was caused by a rare form of electricity in the air. (According to Kant, this same electricity was also responsible for the cat epidemics which had recently broken out in Copenhagen and Vienna.) Such involvement with 'electrical powers' is often associated with schizophrenia.

But Kant was never mad. This was merely

the tight knots which had held him so closely bound throughout his life beginning to loosen. He was fading fast. The few chosen colleagues and favoured students who were invited to dinner would watch in saddened silence as his mind wandered. Then his new servant would lead him away. On 8 October 1803 Kant was ill for the first time in his life. He had a mild stroke after eating too much of his favourite 'English cheese'. After four months of increasing debilitation he died on 12 February 1804. His last words were '*Es ist gut*'. (It is good.) He was buried in the cathedral, his tomb inscribed with the statement that inclined him towards the God he certainly believed in, but never publicly worshipped – words which harked back to an intense small boy listening to a well-meaning mother whom he certainly worshipped: 'The starry heavens above and the moral law within fill the mind with an ever new and increasing admiration and awe, the more often and the more steadily we reflect.'

Afterword

Question: What is Kant's *Critique of Pure Reason* about?

Answer: Metaphysics.

Q: What exactly is metaphysics?

A: This word began as a mistake, and has ended up by being regarded as a mistake. In between times it was the main topic of philosophy.

Q: This still doesn't answer the question. So what precisely does metaphysics mean?

A: Nothing at all, according to most modern philosophers.

Q: Well, what did it originally mean?

A: This word was first used to refer to certain philosophical works of Aristotle. These were the ones which came after his great work on physics, in his collected works. They became known as the 'beyond Physics' works – which in Greek was 'meta-physics'.

Q: But this still doesn't tell me what it means.

A: In these works 'beyond Physics', Aristotle dealt with 'the science of things transcending what is physical or natural'.

Q: And what does that mean?

A: It is the science which deals with the first theoretical principles over and above the physical world. These are the principles which govern our knowledge of that same physical world. In other words, metaphysics deals with whatever transcends the physical world we experience.

Q: But how do we know that there is anything beyond the physical world which we experience?

A: We don't. Which is why most modern philosophers dismiss such metaphysics as a mistake.

Q: But Kant didn't?

A: Kant was determined to create a new metaphysics. Prior to him, Hume had arrived at much the same conclusion as those modern philosophers. Hume thought he had destroyed the possibility of metaphysics.

Q: How?

A: By doubting everything which he couldn't confirm from his own experience.

This extreme scepticism ruled out all kinds of things which humanity had believed in through the centuries, but never actually experienced.

Q: Such as?

A: God, for instance.

Q: But what Hume said didn't seem to make much difference. People still went on believing in God.

A: Yes, but it was now increasingly understood that they did this through a leap of faith, rather than as a result of direct experience or rational argument.

Q: So Hume's 'disproof' of metaphysics didn't make any difference at all?

A: In fact, it made a huge difference. Especially to scientists and philosophers.

Q: How?

A: In ruling out everything except what we can verify through experience, Hume ruled out a lot more than God. More importantly for the scientists and philosophers, he ruled out causality.

Q: How?

A: According to Hume, all we know from

experience is that one thing follows another. We can never know that one thing *causes* another. We cannot go *beyond* our experience and say that. We never actually experience one thing causing another – only one thing following another.

Q: So?

A: This strikes at the heart of all our scientific knowledge. According to Hume, science based on causality is metaphysical – not empirical. It can never be verified. And verification is the very basis of our knowledge. Likewise, philosophy. According to Hume, we can never prove the statements of philosophy, unless they are a result of direct experience.

Q: Such as?

A: Such as the statement: 'This apple is green.'

Q: But that means philosophy can say practically nothing.

A: Precisely. And this is the extreme difficulty which Kant tried to overcome in his philosophy.

Q: How?

A: He tried to show that despite Hume's devastating scepticism, it was still possible to build up a metaphysics. This would be the basis for a universal and logically necessary form of knowledge – which would remain impervious to Hume's scepticism. Kant first set this down in his *Critique of Pure Reason*.

Q: So Kant's metaphysics was an attempt at some kind of ultimate science – which guarantees the truth of our knowledge?

A: Precisely.

Q: And how did he set about this?

A: Kant put forward what he called his 'critical philosophy'. This undertook a profound analysis of epistemology – a study of the very basis on which our knowledge rests. According to Kant, we make certain judgements which are indispensable to all knowledge. These judgements he classified as 'synthetic *a priori*'. By synthetic, he meant they were not analytic, and the knowledge they contained was not implied in the original concept. For instance, 'the ball is round' is an analytic statement – because the concept 'roundness' is contained within the concept 'ball'. However, 'the ball is shiny' is a synthetic judgement. It says something more about the ball than is contained in the original concept, in the same way as an empirical statement. By *a priori*, Kant meant judgements that are necessary and universal. They had to be true *prior* to any experience, and are made by the use of reason alone. Unlike judgements made as a result of experience, they were not particular and contingent. That is, they didn't just apply to one instance and have no logical necessity – such as statements like 'this horse has won the Derby' and 'that horse is brown'.

Like any scientific judgement, these synthetic *a priori* statements had to be undeniable and universally true. In other words, they had to have the same force and strength as an analytic statement, although they were synthetic. And they had to be applicable to experience, whilst at the same time remaining prior to it.

Kant's basic question was: 'How are synthetic *a priori* statements possible?' He now applied this question to mathematics, physics, and metaphysics. According to Kant, mathematics deals with space and time. Kant argued that, contrary to appearances, space and time are in fact *a priori* – that is, they are not part of our experience but a necessary prior condition of that experience. We could have no experience without these 'forms of our sensibility'.

Kant then goes on to argue that statements of physics are *a priori* judgements. They classify empirical judgements (and are thus synthetic), but use concepts which are prior to experience (and are thus *a priori*). These concepts, or 'categories of our understanding' as Kant called them, are much like space and time in mathematics. The 'categories' are the essential framework of our knowledge. They consist of such things as quality, quantity, relation (including causality) and modality (such as existence or non-existence). They are not part of our experience, yet we could not have any experience without them.

However, when we come to metaphysics the opposite is true to mathematics and physics. Metaphysics has nothing to do with experience (as it is 'beyond physics'.) This means we cannot apply 'categories' such as quantity and quality to metaphysics, because these are the framework of our knowledge of *experience*. Thus metaphysics excludes itself from the realm of synthetic *a priori* judgements, and has no scientific basis. So if we take a metaphysical concept, such as God, we cannot make any scientific (or verifiable) statement about him, because any categories which we might apply are only relevant to experience. Thus to talk of the existence (or non-existence) of God is to misapply the categories.

In this way Kant dismissed metaphysics. Yet in doing so he built up his own alternative metaphysical system. The way Kant saw them, the 'forms of our understanding' (space and time), as well as the 'categories of our understanding' (including existence, necessity etc.) are undeniably metaphysical. *We* may consider space and existence to be 'out there' in the physics of our experience, but Kant did not. So his argument against metaphysics applies equally to them. We can make no synthetic *a priori* statements about them. They are not scientific, they are not analytic, and they are not logically necessary: they are metaphysical. And if, on the other hand, they are 'out there' in our experience, they certainly cannot be *a priori* concepts of our understanding.

Kant's *Critique of Practical Reason* attempts to apply a very similar system to ethics. Instead of asking if there are such things as synthetic *a priori* judgements, he asks if there are rules which *a priori* govern our will and can thus claim to be universal. Instead of the categories, he comes up with a 'categorical imperative' – which is not a part of actual moral experience, but the *a priori* framework necessary for it. This categorical imperative he expresses as follows: 'Act only in accord with a principle which you would at the same time will to be a universal law.' Like the categories, this imperative is purely formal. The categories have no empirical content, the categorical imperative has no moral content. This categorical imperative may appear all very well, but it is wide enough to encompass the contradictory moralities of the sado-masochist as well as the peace-and-love hippie. It is also strictly rational and implies that we should regard all human beings as temperamentally identical to ourselves. Our psychology is not strictly rational, and we do not regard others as being temperamentally identical to ourselves. Nor do we wish them to be – unless we happen to be a dictator. How can we even apply such an imperative, if we don't think like this or behave like this? We may subscribe to certain universal principles, but these don't cover all our moral actions. There are certain less fundamental principles which we would have no wish to apply to the moral actions of all peoples. I may abstain from cannibalism, and at the same time wish to see the principle 'eating people is wrong' universally applied. But if I abstain from murder, this does not mean that I wish a policeman to abstain from murdering a murderous hostage-taker.

It is possible to argue that such strictures do not apply, as the categorical imperative is merely the *framework* of morality. By our moral actions we merely *imply* universal principles. But such retreat into formality renders the categorical imperative itself utterly vacuous. It plainly states that we should behave in such a way that we wish all other people to behave.

Key quotations

The following excerpt is from the opening of The Critique of Pure Reason, *where Kant prepares to lay the foundations of his philosophy. As can be seen from the second sentence, Kant begins as he means to go on. Persevere beyond this easily spotted ambush and you will soon become aware of a quality of mind which nimbly transcends the quagmire of its conveyance.*

It is beyond a doubt that all our knowledge begins with experience. For by what should our faculties be roused to act, if not by objects that affect our senses, and thus partly of themselves produce impressions, partly, again, bring the understanding itself into movement, in order to compare these, to join or disjoin them, and in this manner work up such crude material of the intimations of sense into a cognition or recognition of objects which is named experience. So far as time is concerned, then, no cognition of ours precedes experience, and with experience all our knowledge begins.

But, though all our knowledge begins *with* experience, it does not follow that therefore it all derives *from* experience. For it is just possible that experience is itself a compound. It is just possible, that is, that there is experience, besides what is due to the impression of sense, something (when merely acting because of impression); and in that case, it would take long practice, it may be, to enable us to distinguish the latter, and separate it from the former.
Critique of Pure Reason, Introduction, Part 1

He continues his argument: Is there really such a component part of knowledge as is independent of experience, and indeed, of any impression of sense whatever? Such component part of knowledge did it exist, were alone to be termed truly *a priori*; and it would evidently stand in contradistinction to what other component part of knowledge is called empirical: the latter, namely, having its source only *a posteriori*, or in experience.

The expression *a priori*, at the same time is not precise enough to designate the entire sense of the preceding question. For of many a mere empirical fact, we say, that we know it *a priori*, simply because we do not derive it directly from experience, but from a general rule; and this, even notwithstanding that the rule itself may be so derived. For example, we say of a man that shall have undermined his house, he might have known *a priori* that it would fall in; he had no occasion to wait for the experience of the actual event. Nevertheless, he could not have known this absolutely *a priori*. For that bodies are heavy and, consequently, fall when their supports are withdrawn – this, at least, he must have known by experience beforehand.

Ibid., Introduction, Part 1

Kant goes on to explain: We shall understand by cognitions *a priori*, not such as are independent of this or that experience, but such as are totally independent of any experience whatsoever. Opposed to these are empirical cognitions, or such as are only possible *a posteriori*, or from experience. Pure, again, are those *a priori* cognitions which are quite free from all and every empirical admixture. Thus, for example, the proposition, that all change has its cause, is an *a priori* proposition; but it is not, at the same time, *purely* such, for change is an idea which can only be derived from experience.

> *Ibid.*, Introduction, Part 1

The argument continues, and the plot thickens. This extremely rare opportunity to accompany one of the finest intellects in history as it proceeds on its original way should not be missed. To aspire to attain such heights easily, defeats the entire purpose of the exercise:

What is wanted here is a criterion, by means of which we may, with certainty, distinguish what is pure from what is empirical. Now experience informs us that something *is* so and so, but not that it cannot be otherwise. *Firstly*, then, should there be a proposition such that it is thought together with its necessity, then it is a judgement *a priori*; and, if underived from any other, absolutely *a priori*. *Secondly*, experience extends to its judgements never strict or true, but only (through induction) assumptive or comparative universality; so that, properly, it can only be said: So far as we are yet aware, there is no exception to this or that rule. Should any judgement, then, be thought in strict universality, or so, that is, that exceptions are impossible, we may be sure that that judgement is no derivative from experience, but directly *a priori*. Empirical universality, therefore, is only an arbitrary raising of validity from that which obtains in most cases to that which holds good in all, as in the proposition, for example, that all bodies are heavy. Whereas, when strict universality attaches to a judgement, such universality points to a special cognitive source, namely, to a faculty of cognition *a priori*. Necessity and strict universality, therefore, are sure criteria of *a priori* cognition, and inseparably found together. In practice, however, as it is easier, now to apply the one and now the other, it will be advisable to avail ourselves, as occasion may suggest, of either criterion separately; for, even separately, either of them is quite infallible.

Ibid., Introduction, Part 2

Kant now elaborates: It is easy to show that there actually are in our knowledge such necessary and, in the strictest sense, universal (consequently pure *a priori*) judgements. Would we have an example from science, we have only to turn to any proposition in mathematics; while, as for the most ordinary common sense, there is obviously to hand, by way of instance, the proposition that every change must have a cause, where the very notion cause so manifestly implies necessity (of connexion with an effect) and strict universality (of rule), that it would be altogether lost did we derive it, like Hume, from our conjoining what simply follows with what simply precedes, through the mere habit of experience, and the consequent simple custom of connecting ideas (where the necessity could only be subjective). Besides demonstrating the actual existence in our knowledge of principles *a priori* by a reference to fact, we might even *a priori* prove as much. We might demonstrate, that is, the indispensable necessity of such principles to the very possibility of experience. For how should there be any certainty in experience, were all the rules in it only empirical and (consequently) contingent? It were hardly possible, evidently, to allow any such rules the name of first principles. But it may suffice here to have demonstrated the fact of the possession of pure cognition on our part, together with the signs of the latter. Nay, not merely judgements, but even certain ideas, may claim for themselves an *a priori* origin. Suppose, in the case of our empirical idea of a *body*, we successively withdraw all its empirical constituents, such as colour, consistency, weight, even impenetrability, we shall still find it impossible to withdraw the space it occupied. This space will still remain when the body itself has disappeared. In like matter, if, in regard to our empirical idea of an object in general, whether corporeal or incorporeal, we withdraw all properties known to us from experience, we shall still be unable to withdraw from it those by which we think it as substance, or as attributive to substance (though this notion of substance has more determination in it than that of an object in general). We must, therefore, overborne by the necessity with which said notion forces itself upon us, admit that it has its seat *a priori* in our faculties of cognition.

Ibid., Introduction, Part 2

Here Kant explains the notion of Time according to his philosophy:

Time has no objective reality; it is not an accident, not a substance, and not a relation: it is a purely subjective condition, necessary because of the nature of the human mind, which co-ordinates all our sensibilities by a certain law, and is a pure intuition. We co-ordinate substances and accidents alike, according to simultaneity and succession, only through the concept of time.

De Mundi Sensibilis atque intelligibilis forma et principiis, 3, 14.

Here Kant differentiates between different kinds of happiness:

Because someone is only happy insofar as he gratifies a desire, the feeling that causes him to

enjoy such great pleasures, without him need-
ing great ability in order to do so, is certainly
no trivial matter. Fat people, whose favourite
artists are their cooks and whose masterpieces
lie in their cellar, enjoy their common obsceni-
ties and vulgar witticisms just as much as
nobler souls enjoy their more refined pursuits.
An indolent fellow who loves to have books
read aloud to him because he enjoys falling
asleep in this fashion, the businessman who
considers all pleasure a distraction apart from
working out his profits on a smart business
deal, someone who loves the opposite sex for
the sheer pleasure of it and nothing else, the
keen hunter whether he merely hunts flies like
the Roman Emperor Domitian or ferocious
beasts like A— – all these have feelings which
make them capable of experiencing pleasure in
their own way, without them being envious of
others or even being capable of conceiving of
other pleasures. This kind of feeling, which can
take place without any thought at all, I shall
completely disregard.

His argument continues:

Fine feeling, which I shall now consider, is for the most part of two kinds: the feeling of the sublime and that of the beautiful. Each gives us pleasure, but in different ways. The sight of a snow-capped mountain peak rising above the clouds, the description of a wild storm, or Milton's depiction of the kingdom of hell – each of these gives us joy, but mingled with terror. On the other hand, the sight of flower-covered meadows, valleys with winding streams and grazing flocks, the description of Elysium, or Homer's depiction of the girdle of Venus, these also give us a pleasant sensation, but one that is joyful and happy. In order to feel the former sensation we must have a *feeling of the sublime*, but in order to experience the latter properly we must have a *feeling of the beautiful*.

'Of the Beautiful and the Sublime', Section 1, paras 2 & 3

A rare example of Kantian poetry. This was written in 1782 on the occasion of the death of Pastor Lilienthal, who had married Kant's parents:

> *Was auf das Leben folgt deckt tiefe Finsterniss;*
> *Was uns zu thun gebuhrt, dess sind wis nur gewiss.*

What comes after life is hidden in deep darkness;
What we are expected to do, that alone we know.

The following goes a long way towards explaining the popularity of Kant's geography lectures with the citizens of Königsberg. It was written by Dr J. H. Stirling, a nineteenth-century British member of the Philosophical Society of Berlin.

[In Kant's geography lectures] he cannot help referring to some of the most interesting facts that have reached him ... Negroes are born white, all to a ring around the navel. The ibis dies the moment it quits Egypt. The lion is so

noble, he will not put a paw upon a woman
... The water at the Cape is so pure that it
remains sweet when brought to Europe. If
you make a cup of the rhinoceros's horn, any
poison will splinter it ... In the Canary
Islands there is the tree of life that never rots,
whether in ground or in water. There is a
mussel in Italy that gives out so much light,
that you can read by it. In Languedoc there
is a hot spring that hatches eggs ... Wild
beasts only eat Negroes in Gambia, and leave
Europeans alone. The Negroes in America are
immensely fond of dog's flesh, and all the
dogs bark at them.

*According to Dr Stirling, these views were 'all
gravely propounded'.*

Chronology of significant philosophical dates

6th century BC	The start of Western philosophy with Thales of Miletus.
end of 6th century BC	Death of Pythagoras.
399 BC	Socrates sentenced to death in Athens.
c.387 BC	Plato founds the Academy in Athens, the first university.
335 BC	Aristotle founds the Lyceum in Athens, rival school to the Academy.
324 AD	Emperor Constantine moves capital of Roman Empire to Byzantium.
400 AD	St Augustine writes his

Confessions.
Philosophy absorbed into
Christian theology.

410 AD   Sack of Rome by Visigoths
              heralds start of Dark Ages.

529 AD   Closure of Academy in Athens
              by Emperor Justinian marks
              end of Hellenic thought.

mid 13th   Thomas Aquinas writes his
century   commentaries on Aristotle. Era
              of Scholasticism.

1453   Fall of Byzantium to Turks,
              end of Byzantine Empire.

1492   Columbus reaches America.
              Renaissance in Florence and
              revival of interest in Greek
              learning.

1543   Copernicus publishes *De
              revolutionibus orbium
              caelestium* (On the Revolution
              of the Celestial Orbs) proving
              mathematically that the earth
              revolves around the sun.

1633   Galileo forced by Church to
            recant heliocentric theory of
            the Universe.

1641   Descartes publishes his
            Meditations, the start of
            modern philosophy.

1677   Death of Spinoza allows
            publication of his *Ethics*.

1687   Newton publishes *Principia*,
            introducing concept of gravity.

1689   Locke publishes *Essay
            Concerning Human
            Understanding*. Start of
            Empiricism.

1710   Berkeley publishes *Principles
            of Human Knowledge*,
            advancing Empiricism to new
            extremes.

1716   Death of Leibnitz.

1739–40   Hume publishes *Treatise of
            Human Nature*, taking
            Empiricism to its logical
            limits.

1781   Kant, woken from his 'dogmatic slumbers' by Hume, publishes *Critique of Pure Reason*. Great era of German metaphysics begins.

1807   Hegel publishes *The Phenomenology of Mind*: high point of German metaphysics.

1818   Schopenhauer publishes *The World as Will and Representation*, introducing Indian philosophy into German metaphysics.

1889   Nietzsche, having declared 'God is dead', succumbs to madness in Turin.

1921   Wittgenstein publishes *Tractatus Logico-Philosophicus*, claiming the 'final solution' to the problems of philosophy.

1920s   Vienna Circle propound Logical Positivism.

1927   Heidegger publishes *Sein und Zeit* (Being and Time), heralding split between analytical and continental philosophy.

1943   Sartre publishes *L'Être et le néant* (Being and Nothingness), advancing Heidegger's thought and instigating Existentialism.

1953   Posthumous publication of Wittgenstein's *Philosophical Investigations*. High era of Linguistic Analysis.